Perspectives
Space Exploration
Is It Worth It?

Flying Start
to Literacy®

Contents

Introduction

Should we continue to explore space?

Space exploration has led to incredible inventions. It has facilitated massive growth in our knowledge and use of technology, and it has inspired people around the globe to unite in a common cause. Why would we ever stop?

Because the cost of space exploration is enormous, travelling into space is dangerous and there are problems on Earth that we should solve first.

So what do you think? Do the benefits of space exploration outweigh the arguments against it?

In awe of space

Christina Burke Broderick has been interested in space for as long as she can remember.

Do you share her passion? When you look up at the night sky, what do you think about?

I've been interested in space ever since I can remember. When I was younger, I had stickers of stars and planets all around my room; they glowed above my bed when I turned off my lights.

Now, I've learnt more about the planets at school, and about stars and comets and galaxies and black holes. Even with all this learning, I know there is still so much left to know. I could study the universe for a million years and still know only a tiny bit of everything there is to discover! Even scientists, who dedicate their whole lives to outer space, don't know what makes up 95 per cent of the universe.

The wider universe is exciting and new. For me, it is filled with more opportunities for science and discovery than anything on Earth. We live on a tiny planet in a massive cosmos. There are only eight planets in our solar system, and even these remain mostly a mystery to us. And beyond our solar system, there is an infinite number of new and undiscovered planets. Most of space has never even been seen by a person, let alone touched – or explored!

The universe is expanding all the time. Scientists don't know how, but every second it stretches out farther. There are infinite possibilities out there.

I want to know what lies beyond everything we know about the universe. I want to see new planets and discover the answers to the big questions about how our universe works. To challenge the boundaries of what humans know is, I believe, how the future will be created – and how humanity will forge a place in this future.

Focus on Earth, not Space

A program to send humans to Mars could cost hundreds of billions of dollars. For that amount of money, we could end world hunger — and much more, argues Joshua Hatch.

What do you think is more important: spending money on space travel and exploration or ending world hunger, housing the homeless and finding cures for deadly diseases?

Exploring space is like buying fancy jewellery. It's a luxury. Sending humans, or even robots, into space doesn't put food in people's mouths or shelter the homeless.

Just like families living on a budget, society must set priorities. We shouldn't spend money on space until we've solved more important problems. Imagine if instead of buying groceries, your family bought fancy watches. What good would all those watches be if you and your family are hungry?

And there are many problems on Earth that require our attention. We need to address climate change. We should better fund cancer research. We could house the homeless. There are people around the globe who don't even have working toilets.

Shouldn't we address more immediate issues before we build multimillion-dollar rockets? Why should we shortchange those problems to send a few people into space?

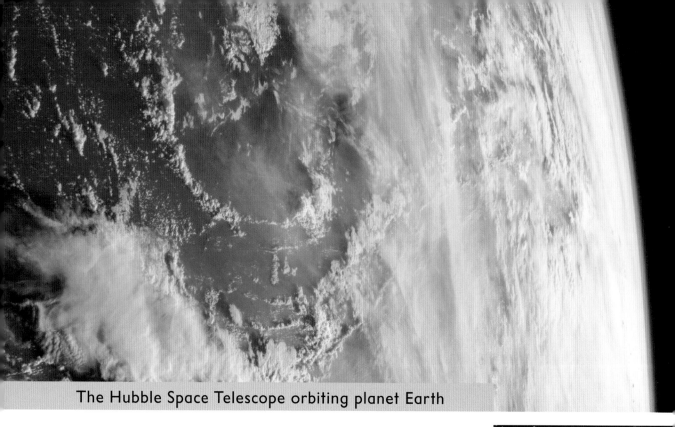

The Hubble Space Telescope orbiting planet Earth

Money isn't the only issue involved. A lot of really smart people spend their time thinking about how to safely send people to space and bring them home. What if those smart people were working on more important problems instead? Maybe we would have already found a cure for cancer!

Sure, space is cool. The photos from Mars Exploration Rovers and the Hubble Space Telescope are amazing. Some awesome technology has come from the US space program, but some of those innovations may have been more interesting than important. Humans survived for thousands of years without communications, weather or GPS satellites. They're nice luxuries, but they're not necessary.

At the end of the day, going into space costs too much and diverts resources from the many problems that require our immediate attention on Earth. Millions of people around the globe will suffer from serious illnesses. They could go hungry. They might lose their jobs or homes.

Maybe once we fix things on Earth, then we can explore space. But until then, let's invest in ourselves before we shoot money at the stars.

A Mars Rover

Exploring space:

The benefits to us

Space exploration is costly, but it is a smart investment, writes journalist Claire Halliday. The benefits of spending money on space exploration are not immediately apparent. But in time, the effort will lead to a better understanding of planet Earth, as well as space.

Are you persuaded by Claire's argument? Why or why not?

See Earth from a fresh perspective

By studying Earth from space, scientists and climate-change specialists learn more about our planet's climate and weather systems.

When they measure and compare scientific data over a period of time, scientists have more information and can make better decisions about how we can take action to make the differences that will benefit all human life – now and in the future.

An investment in a safer future

Thanks to space exploration, we now enjoy many inventions that have improved our lives. We have satellites that help support the beaming of TV and radio, the Internet and GPS navigation around the globe.

Our health has also been improved. Did you know that new water and air-filtration systems that keep us safe and healthy were a direct result of the need to create fresh water and air for astronauts exploring our universe?

And we benefitted from life-changing medical advances. Many of the parts that are used in the design and manufacture of artificial limbs were developed for space vehicles. These discoveries led to the use of diamond coatings that make joints last longer, as well as special foams that make prosthetics feel more comfortable.

Devices that help people who suffer breathing difficulties have also been helped by space-exploration research. It has helped to make firefighters' protective breathing masks lighter and easier to wear.

Safer car tyres is another benefit of space exploration. The National Aeronautics and Space Administration (NASA) in partnership with a chemical company created a material that is stronger than steel and good at absorbing sudden shocks. Tyre manufacturers further developed this material to create tyres that last longer by almost 200,000 kilometres!

Survival of our species

Climate change continues to negatively impact our world. Exploring whether life can exist on Mars is a way to find answers to important questions about the way Earth's ecosystem works. It provides information about what we can do to protect Earth.

Space has no borders; it's a place where parts of the world can unite in a common goal. When humanity makes a global commitment to explore space – to the best of our current resources and abilities – our society is making a commitment to an exciting future.

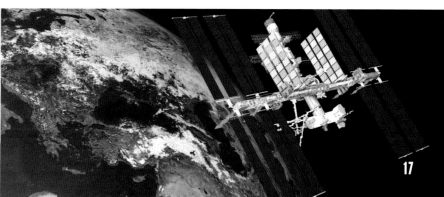

Earth from space

What does this make you think?

How does it make you feel?

Space junk

Since 1957, humans have put thousands of satellites into orbit. But they don't last forever. These objects keep circling around the earth, even when they break or stop working. They become space junk, and it's getting a bit crowded in space, writes Charlene Brusso.

How can we control space junk? Who is responsible?

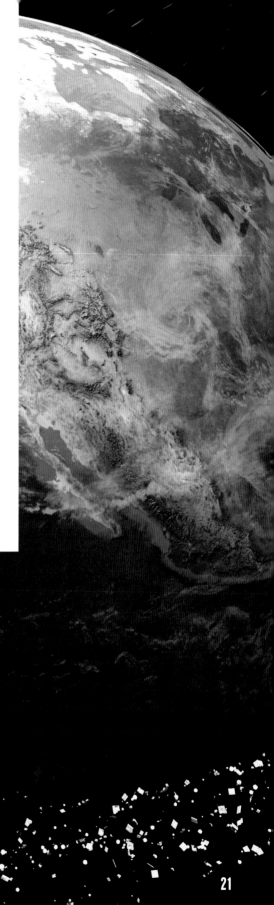

3... 2... 1...

The white dots around this Earth picture show just some of the thousands of human-made objects orbiting our planet. Only about 10 per cent of these dots is a working satellite. The rest are old satellites, parts of rockets and other debris.

All of this space junk is moving at thousands of kilometres an hour. At that speed, even a tiny screw is dangerous – it can punch a hole right through a spacecraft. Sometimes, bits of space junk collide or explode, shattering into thousands of smaller pieces. The more crowded space gets, the more likely collisions become.

Solving the problem of space junk

Space agencies have traffic computers that keep track of 22,000 big pieces of space junk. The computers warn spacecraft to move if it looks like something might hit it.

Meanwhile, scientists around the world are trying to think of ways to clean up old satellites. There are many ideas. Most involve slowing junk down and pulling it towards Earth. Once the object hits Earth's atmosphere, friction will cause it to burn up safely.

Self-destruct satellites

The easiest way to keep space clean is to build satellites to dispose of themselves. When the satellite is no longer needed, it will fire a thruster or open a solar sail. The satellite will then slow and fall towards Earth. This approach could help eliminate space junk in the future.

The RemoveDebris satellite launch from the International Space Station

RemoveDebris is one of many ideas for junk-collecting satellites. It involves both a net and a harpoon to catch stray junk and reel it in. Attaching a sail or thruster then slows the junk down so it spirals towards Earth. The satellite uses a laser to scan the junk to decide how best to deal with it.

RemoveDebris is already being tested at the International Space Station. Scientists are targeting the largest pieces of junk first. They want to get them out of the way before they break up into more pieces of junk.

Space blanket

One of the most unusual ideas is a thin, bendy, solar-powered spacecraft that looks like a blanket. NASA's Brane Craft will seek out a bit of space space junk, wrap around it and then power itself down to burn up in the atmosphere. So we might need many of these spacecraft.

What is your opinion? How to write a persuasive argument

1. State your opinion

Think about the issues related to your topic. What is your opinion?

2. Research

Research the information you need to support your opinion.

Related *Perspectives* book   Internet   Other sources

3. Make a plan

Introduction

How will you "hook" the reader?

State your opinion.

List reasons to support your opinion.

What persuasive devices will you use?

Reason 1
Support your reason
with evidence and details.

Reason 2
Support your reason
with evidence and details.

Reason 3
Support your reason
with evidence and details.

Conclusion

Restate your opinion. Leave your reader with a strong message.

4. Publish

Publish your persuasive argument.

Use visuals to reinforce your opinion.